CALIFORNIA COLLEGE OF ARTS AND CRAFTS
WITHDRAWN
THE LIBRARY

ALSO BY WALTER BENTON

THIS IS MY BELOVED

THIS IS A BORZOI BOOK

PUBLISHED IN NEW YORK

BY ALFRED A. KNOPF

NEVER A GREATER NEED

NEVER A GREATER NEED

BY WALTER BENTON

ALFRED A. KNOPF *NEW YORK*
1963

Manufactured in the United States of America and distributed by Random House, Inc. Published in Canada by Random House of Canada, Limited.

Published February 9, 1948
Reprinted eight times
Tenth printing, April 1963

THIS IS A BORZOI BOOK,
PUBLISHED BY ALFRED A. KNOPF, INC.

Several of these poems have appeared in Poetry, Esquire, Fantasy, *and* The Saturday Review of Literature.

Most of the poems in part V were composed before 1942. Those in parts I and IV were written in Europe.

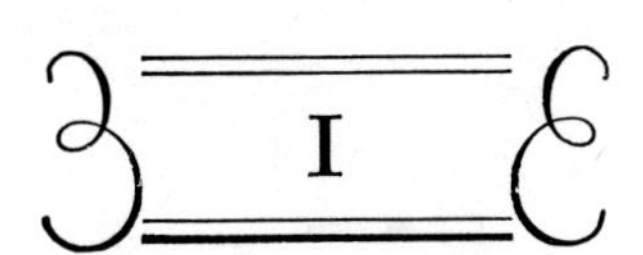

Notes for a Letter

1 :

It rained last night . . . passing through an old
stone-mouldy village —

small, spring rain . . . like the rain another night,
a war ago —
(the great blue starry bubble night)
the misting, Maryland night, we rediscovered love.

I write this because
of the ever green garden of days and nights like that
in the small light cloud just above my eyes —

and because tonight,
after another lost day and a profitless mailcall,
I wish-thought this to you:

that each night's love you lay aside for my return.

O then . . . across the oceans and continents would be
barely the length of your awaiting arms —
for you are my anthem and my flag,
my creed, my country . . . and what is left of God!

2 :

The crazed moth like a wild wilful girl
drums against the unyielding authority of the glittering mirror,
pounds myriad fists against the sunlight of the bulbs.

Neither fatigue nor veronal taking . . . I have lain
most of the night seeing you,
possessing you in detail . . . without subtlety or continence,
reserve or moderation — without discretion, without rest.

You are on my mind . . . immense as only need and loneliness
conceive a woman —
you are in my eyes, my nostrils . . . you are wonderfully
heavy in my arms with the sweet heaviness of one
long and well loved.

Your breasts snug cheek to cheek like the breasts
of two white pigeons
forever face me . . . bearing small roses. Your pale thighs

curve smile upon smile —
your hips full filled as a goatskin of wine flood my personal world
with scents and colors . . . like a tropical garden.

You are on my mind — abundant, elemental . . . a spreading jungle
edging out logic and corrupting God,
folding me . . . drawing me deep into ecstatic darkness —
filling me with heady warmth like the taste of impassioned lips.

O I have passed this night face pressed against
the window to heaven —
like a starved kid big-eyeing the rich man's table.

3 :

Juxtaposition of the ballooned fatigues the Pacific
laps up some cursed beach
with great gathering clumsy hands like a bashful lover —

and you, alive . . . water-spanked pink, sweet lake water
flowing smoothly around your elongated thighs,
nipping your tightened teats and multiplying your dimples —

is like a tabloid's composite headline of murder and love.

But as men wade ashore some islet meant for a picnic only
to die on the sunny sand meant best for building castles,
love enters the frantic mind

often . . . inexplicably as a child toddling out
into heavy traffic —
and nearly everyone in his last spare moment will pause to pick it up.

And it is wonderful, like feeling sudden pain in a paralyzed body.

4:

Spring came this year . . . and spring is gone.
Like the Cinderella princes . . . like the one and only
met turning a corner at the Mardi Gras — and I

too starry eyed to ask her name,
to lift the anonymous mask — to slay the guarding lover-dragon.

Forever and ever gone, taking her eyes, her smile,
carrying away in her soft arms
nights and nights of love . . . kisses and kisses in her mouth.

I only know of spring the small white fragrant bells you loved,
tall slender forsythias —
jonquils with yellow honeyed throats . . . to bring you:

I only know of spring the bright,
the pastel green . . . the russet patterned cottons you wear —
the first sun lighting your winter-white body cyclamen-pink:

I only know of spring the graceful indolence of you
lying relaxed,
arms free where they fall . . . legs loose, unashamed —

like one having just freely given of her love . . . with hardly a kiss
left on her lips —
your face small like a girl's first valentine upon the pillow.

II

1 : It Was a Late May Weekend . . . Remember ?

I came in from camp and you from the city . . . uncertain,
apprehensive still —
having for days rehearsed, each by his own script, the play

of attitudes and words, the first tentative touch,
the implied yes
and (always) the ultimate embrace.
But as it happened: I took your hand to cross the street,

and our fingers held . . . the way vines do in growing,
and we were wonderfully inarticulate —
we were breathlessly afraid . . . like flying in a dream.

Then most of the afternoon we lay in the sun,
among the last late dandelions and curious foraging ants —
shuttling secret thoughts between us
and exquisite promises . . . anticipating evening.

2 : As the Night Whitens into Day

This morning . . . after the war and everything
(at the end of the sixth day of God's anger and the madness of man)
promises take shape . . . become.

How much lovelier you are than any!
Your flesh is of the pale cloth of the moon . . . and its fragrance is sweet-clean as a sunned linen.

Ah, darling . . . as the night whitens into day,
we have loved and slept, bathed and returned to one another —
marveling at the wondrous things we are.

All your incomparable body laughs to my touch,
opens like the roses upon which warm rain has fallen.

O there is no drink like the cup your kisses fill —
there is no peace like the sleep shaped by our love's violence!

3 : We Are Well Again

This leopard lightness that powers us . . . idle or in motion,
this dreamless sleep
that flows through insulated valleys till all the clocks run down —
bespeak complete accord of mind and body . . . and of circumstance.

Hotel becomes a home by the witchery of your presence,
you fill the threadbare room as a songbird fills an empty orchard
upon spring.
You endow the warped bed . . . the one, two chairs —
the rug's frayed edges spread peacock feathers under your feet.

Depart . . . and you tilt the firmament! Near me, however,
no step or gesture places you out of place, disturbs the balance.
The room gathers around you —
the looking glass embraces you with endearing perspectives.

And seeing yourself loved in my eyes and wanted . . . you strut
like a favorite to wild applause, tempting me with the choicest
blossoms of your most secluded garden.

4: And Spring Returns

There is none like you . . . I have loved before —
even as you . . . and believed each story's ending inconceivable
without certain death to follow as night follows day.

But here we are, deep in each other's eyes . . . like children
in an unfolding fairy tale — and no less credulous.

The years have altered nothing . . . dulled the senses
nor discredited the magic:
our moon will ever be a swarm of silver locust on a ruffled sea —
our stars will be loud and many as autumn starlings.

Be glad as I am glad, for we have learned that love recurs,
richer for its fallow interval.
The nightingale
sings no less wondrously this night for having sung another.

And need I say that I have known no sweeter lips than yours
nor ever wakened to a brighter morning than this beside you?
See, my touch is as forever first —
I enter breathless as a frightened thief stealing into a church.

5 : Of Your Infinite Aspects

You ask if you have changed: you have.
As a lover's kiss evokes . . . evolves . . . shapes into a child,
so do you move from beauty to beauty —
as a white pear blossom evolves into a golden pear.

And who will choose between a thing of fragrant petals
and one of honeyed curves . . . for beauty's face?
And as for other delights —
where once the bee sucked sweet . . . now sucks the wasp.

You vary to fit the revelations of love
as the ermine varies to fit the seasons —

awed, reverent love . . . white as a nun's, fleshless as
the miracle temples mad saints invoke;
ruddy, riotous love —
hairy and incontinent as the compensatory dreams of the lonely;

gentle, lasting love; compelling, brief, total as a trance;
sustaining as a prayer and our daily bread;
skilled, practiced love; tentative love curious children play —
when each move reveals some strange and secret wonder.

We are two vines curved to one another . . . twined into
one stem —
too like and near to discern the changes of our growing.

6 : Manhattan

Spring sits on the city like a hen on a doorknob.
Birth cannot swell stone seed-leaves apart,
split the macadam shell —
carpeting the traffic valleys green from river to river.

Nevertheless . . . the small rain upon the unresponsive pavement
is no less wonderful to walk in
than the rain falling on young wheat . . . and unlocking orchards.

The ascending sun looms higher than the skyscrapers, enters
the tenements . . . like an angel with bright tidings,
lights the cavernous streets — humanizing the nether dwellers.

Low over the Hudson, the sunflower moon . . . pearl-luminous
as the Carib moon — and technicolored
as a blonde asleep under a sunlamp . . . or a nude by Renoir.

But I knew spring in you even before the thundering
tongues of the sky proclaimed it
and the avenue windows styled it . . . I saw its awakening

many a morning in your own long, unhurried awakening,
in your slowed walk . . . and your quickened love — I could tell
when near you
by the subtle musk of you . . . like freshly turned earth.

Yes . . . before the roofgardens stirred and the backyards budded
your mouth was red clover and your breasts were white,
not of the cool nun whiteness of lily or narcissus, but milk-white warm
like blossoming plum.

7 : You Among Flowers

The butterfly weed in the terra-cotta vase recalls
the Ozarks . . . Taneycomo Lake —
and above all,
its coralline sparks against the milkweed milk of your throat and shoulders,
storming the gentle brown of your eyes and hair.

You always held flowers so . . . in the sheltering curve
of your left arm,
as a child is held — the blossoms miniature copies of your face.

You were loveliest when your face matched small spring flowers,
wild grown, peasant bonneted —
such as it hurts to pick . . . and hurts to leave alone.

But when you blossomed out variegated, hot-house gardened,
your beauty troubled me —
I saw you a jewel burning in each stalking eye . . . and sensed
you were not wholly mine, like a star or a people's song.

8 : Jones Beach

The sun is hot, the water cool . . . you resist the delightful
shock like a girl her first love,
giving little and moving out of reach — toes first . . . then more.

The sea, more resolute than you, lassoes you with a wave,
and you are in.
Then you toddle out on your exhausted hothouse legs,
and the warm sun covers you.

And while our corned flesh burns brightly on the sand,
the Atlantic tips, topples, breaks,
loud-muffled as the mad mind's pulse. Over and over . . . the blue
windlifted hills,
the onset of the sky . . . the near horizon rising, ebbing.

Love is a burden if you cannot give it, O hoarded love
is heavy to bear. Around us . . . everywhere
sun-drenched, sea-scented women . . . carrying love,
holding it high as an offering . . . hugging it as a pampered child.

Their sun-ripe thighs inexhaustibly laden —
their expert arms rehearse on water their sweet curving.

Priceless among the polished shells, seaweed and the junked
armor of the horseshoe crab — they lie,
each with an empty paradise inside her . . . waiting for God to walk in.

9 : Northern Lights (July 26, 1946)

Lo, the radiant hand prongs forth coronally into space !

From what nether world ray out its green-gray fingers,
sunflowering the night like the whirling hand of Van Gogh ?

And you half sleeping beside me on the tall roof above
the still city, among the terrorized stars —
dreamily spacing words of wondrous inconsequence.

O the kisses of your mouth blot out the luminous
brilliance of heaven —
and your arms around me are garlands of young roses !

See, the agitation of the sky subsides each time we move
together . . . as if in wonder —
there is no room in all of time for more than moments of this.

10 : The Sublet

When the banishing archangel comes with his flaming sword
in mid-September,
where will I take you in this star-set tent that is our land ?

Stand by me at the window, darling . . . and look down
on the lesser Edens.
See how the cloud-induced twilight deepens the colors of the city —

stressing the blue of the awnings, animating the green
shutters, roof gardens,
purpling the skyscraper's gray . . . like distant hills.

Now rain comes . . . how beautiful is rain to the sheltered !
The air shall be bright cellophane,
it shall be as the glass-green air of the forest.
The washed-red brick . . . the verdigris of the watertower roofs.

Your hand finds mine . . . I turn —
Ah, you are the harbor
of my voyage, the shore and the garden,
you are the sky of my stars and the sleep of my dreaming.

I shall measure off all that my arms encompass of you
and it shall be my home —
your mouth shall be my meat and drink . . . your arms my white bed.

11 : *Twenty-one Stories to Heaven*

If you lean far enough out . . . you can see both rivers.
And the tight casement crowds us irresistibly into a kiss
that snuffs out daylight —
lights the stars, the candles . . . fashions an altar.

And we forget the window-eyes below aspiring to you —
surely some poet's arms reach up,
some young adoring priest's . . . envisioning Madonnas.

On yonder aerialed tenement a boy passes a bamboo pole
like a magic wand over the roof . . . and a cloud of pigeons
bursts upwards —
shattering the ceramic sky into fragments, blue and gray.

The pigeons close, descend, alight . . . mending the sky —
like a motion film of an explosion projected in reverse.

O if I could toss handfulls of birds thus into the blue
around you,
you would be beautiful and real among many wings —
a Raphael, a Botticelli fresco in a Renaissance cathedral.

12 : Walking Saturday Afternoon

Alone, I may have long ago withdrawn into the semi-darkness
of a bar:
together, we crowd from window to gaudy window
eagerly like children round a Christmas tree or at a picnic —

unconcerned with the sun, the people, the taxicab horns,
exclusive . . . insulated,
prodigal with words . . . profound words or illogical,
words of the impossible, words of small consequence or none —

Yes —
    you love white brick houses with blue shutters and blue
brick houses with whitewashed shutters,
stables made over, oak beams, tall ceilings, and stone fireplaces:

you have heard me indulgently on asters and water lilies,
atomic war and Hindu poets —
and I know exactly the chaise-longue and the scarlet screens,
Wedgwood and Persian sandals you would have . . . when we are rich.

We have been hours walking, we have seen everything and more —
it is good growing tired together, the sinews
and the senses concurring . . . like a preview of gathering years.

13 : Fourteenth Street

Deep-muffled guttural of the Interborough somewhere
abruptly reminds us the world is more than you and I walking home
in the cool and quiet near-dawn of the city —
shatters the encompassing bubble of our splendid loneliness.

Leisurely, then . . . savoring the antiseptic smell of the tide —
we walk as one,
we cross, regarding the thinning stars more than the traffic,
touching always at some point like magnetized dolls in a dance.

I think to you and you smile in reply, the telepathic wires
shuttling melody between us —
surging exultation like laughing children riding the carousel.

We need no words, we are complete . . . serene as the ultimate
heaven of the Hindu.
Your hand closes upon mine as we take the stairway.

The evening has been very wonderful, we are sleepy and tired —
good night . . . and your arms move around me,
your lips are as the meat of sweet plums.

14 : Intimation of Autumn

I saw immense chrysanthemums today — chrysanthemums and pink
dahlias . . . rose-marble dahlias and amber
chrysanthemums in the porcelain gardens behind glass fences —

pumpkins and maize on staged fields and pheasants in toy camps
in the fable woods . . . behind glass fences.
Is there a surer sign of autumn, except the wild geese flying ?

It has been a lovely summer on the beaches of the city roofs.
What idler on what private shore
can match the harvest colors of your sun-stained thighs ?

Compare . . . hold the ripe berries here, the apples there —
you could lie among the leaves and late flowers in any garden,
and a butterfly would light upon you . . . and feel secure.

See for yourself if your breasts are not whiter than the silver
birch.
The shape of your face shows up the flaws
in the nearly perfect heart-shape of the morning glory leaf.

And what can I say of your mouth that unlike perishable flowers
opens like kisses at all times
of night and day . . . and is certainly most sweet in all seasons ?

15 : *Yellow and White Chrysanthemums Are Green*

Yellow roses are yellow . . . like sulphur or sunflowers,
but yellow chrysanthemums are green, watered-gold green,
like yellow green lemons.

And white chrysanthemums are white like a green-lined
waterfall, while rust or russet are
like no other color of brush or garden . . . only chrysanthemums.

Some grow small plain faces like daisies. These shall I
remember longer than any.
They blossomed till late October in the Blue Ridge Maryland —

and on clear crisp afternoons when the thin mountain air
meant morning frost,
I cut great bouquets to fill our vases, jars, and teapots —
and they smelled caustic-clean in our shabby rented rooms.

III

1 : Snapshot of a Loved Face

This then is you . . . tender-eyed, nineteen . . . mine.
Dear wonder-wide eyes,
dear mouth, O young rose mouth of songs and remembered kisses !

Sweet mouth, whose whispering like tiny feathers in my ear
often excited
sleep into passionate waking . . . lulled waking into sleep.

How luminous your eyes . . . serene as a mountain morning !
I stand wrapt in their warmth as a vain woman in a silken garment,
and it feels good —
it is the smile and the sun,
inside and over me . . . it is all smile and the warm spring sun.

Had you remained as constant as this image . . . mine as then !
I wonder . . . would the stars have spun, clicking off years
as ever,
would men have died and cities crumbled and nations perished —

or would we be walking through green perennial gardens
till time ran out and lights went off
and all was silence,
leaving just you and me, in a still strange land,
like two who do not die but move . . . to be together and alone ?

Now that your intemperance has cancelled mine . . . fully,
act for act and word for bitter word,
achieving reciprocity in scorn and balance in betrayal —

with yes and no for every no and yes . . . and a dead draw
in grievances (fancied or experienced),
only this residue remains:
drab, chronic, hangover days . . . lonely, sterile nights.

And we self-caught in this equation of zeros, pass time
passively —
our nerve-wiring insulated against pleasure and pain alike.

Sometimes we may seek each other in substitute arms —
use love,
wear its mask to please a habit or to incarnate a memory.

Sometimes you may half-waken, perhaps . . . and dream-beguiled
reach out to find —
not me . . . or finding someone, call him by my name.

Sometimes . . . I may walk Eighth Street or Fifty-seventh,
Madison or Fifth,
window-shopping florists and Chinese shops . . . pricing old silver —

or stop at the corner tavern by the East River . . . where
one war-weekend evening
we stopped . . . and the stevedores bought us drinks.

We may even wonder furtively, remaining steadfast, however,
against insinuating irresolutions.
Confide in bartenders, instead . . . or talk to ourselves, agreeing
that all is for the best, that we are right —
that no better way exists than strangling what is left of love.

3 : December 5, 1946

Tonight I think of you with great tenderness.
My dear . . . O my lost !
I sweep aside the rubble of our years to see you clear of their shadow.

Tonight I remember you without passion . . . tenderly —
as a runaway child is recalled on the eve of Christmas.

Ah, love have we known . . . sung love and cursed,
spring love Ohio-deep in hills and lilac, crocuses and dreams —
and winter in a drab Manhattan flat.

We cut across beliefs and customs, we by-passed rules —
scorning the wisest counsels and perjuring ourselves
to stay love when it would go . . . or end it when it tarried.

But tonight . . . tonight, all I remember is:
exactly years ago you entered the deep, the unknown forest of me —
and great bells rang like sunrise Easter morning.

4: On the Eve of 1947

With four and some years lost playing war . . . cancel another.
Cross out a year of seasons, of nights and mornings —
a wasted year
of radio and movie evenings . . . Sundays of pointless solitaire.

And this . . . the richest of our expectant time,
with youth enough still to be strong and years just right to be
wiser than we really are —
and never a greater need for the therapy of love !

We built a house and locked ourselves out.
We kindled a fire and sought chance firesides for warmth.
We lighted a lamp then followed jack-o'-lantern in the night.

I wonder . . . some late day, when all your world
has shrunk into a pinch of dust between a miser's fingers —
will remembering comfort you, my dear ?

The worst is the way days come and go.
And the clocks hurry their circles of time touching all things.

And much that is young or green yellows or ages.
And much that is beautiful or fresh turns . . . passes one way or another.
And much that is whole dissolves past all recognition.

The season's metamorphosis begins. The last of winter lies dark on the land.
The crows are restless in the treetops. Spring will be early.

6 : And Spring Again

Such things I remember now it is spring and you are gone !
Daily . . . unnoticed-till-absent things,
like air or heart's beating —

words that would pass neither for wit nor wisdom . . . or acts for grace,
pebbles underfoot the polishing of years makes jewels of.
You might as well be here.

After the sterile loneliness of winter
the sunned earth has flowered out with dark paleozoic fertility.
Remember the longstemmed tiger
and lemon lilies in the regenerated stripmined backyards of Joplin,

the ever wilting daisies and violets we vowed never to pick,
the barbed lavender thistles you loved . . . but I had to carry —
the dew the blossoms and the leaves
imparted to your arms, emphasizing their pubescent softness ?

You were wary of bees, mostly . . . I, of ivy and of sumac,
as we trespassed, field to field, until you tired and grew gently
will-less —
glad of my arms each time a fence or an excavation challenged us.

Then I was strong . . . and always held you longer than it took
to help you over.
O it was good feeling you mine completely . . . certain that all was yes
and no was inarticulate in your lips and limbs.

Where will it be then I shall rediscover you . . . all over,
when we have crossed the coma of night —
what page of what story,
a line of what song or poem . . . what phrase of remembered music?

Our ways have not always paralleled, we have appointed
no X hill or crossroad,
no unmistakable landmark, like a star or a lighthouse —
no absolute hour . . . like high noon or the curfew hour.

It may be we shall meet on a trackless outskirt of the land,
on a path too narrow to pass each other by —
or a thronged thoroughfare . . . where the harassed mind
blacks out against the sea of faces, retreats into non-recognition.

A street recalled . . . revisited, a nameless beach,
a deserted downtown corner Sunday morning . . . or Times Square
at 12:01 of a brand new year. A masquerade,
when with the last late dance and dancers lift their masks.

Or will we simply waken side by side one day like disenchanted
lovers in a legend,
beautiful with sleep and whole with love —
remembering only the last long parting of our lips before
sleep took us away from one another . . . each into his own body.

IV

1

This poem is for those
who died unarmed, bewildered . . . behind high-voltage fences,
behind barbed wire fences or dark impenetrable walls,
who died slowly and dully, with days and weeks and years of dying —

the peasant Pole and the fishermen Greek, the Norseman
and the Russian,
the Jew, the Frenchman, the Yugoslav, the Czech . . . the German —

the parachuted flier, the cut-off doughboy,
the surrendered poilu, the captured Tommy, or the wounded Red —

this is for the slave worker dying when he could work no longer,
the idealist, when he dared to dream a better world;
the wise man, dead for his wisdom incompatible with murder,
the freeman, for his freedom,
the good man, for his God . . . the colored man, for his color —

this is for the guerrilla and the partisan,
the Maquis, the ELAS, the Loyalist . . . the saboteur —

this is for the little nobody-people who got in the way and died
without glory or hope,
without food . . . or weapons in their hands,
without a hearing or a trial . . . without sense, without reason,
without medicine or God, without the Last Sacrament —

for whom there will be no marble chiseled, no copper hammered
in their tortured images,
no crosses, stars, commemorative stamps or purple ribbons —

because they died as Christ may have died
at the hands of more expert, more calculating murderers,
and because they were many million . . . mostly poor.

2

Who knows their names ?

What was their work ?

Which was a peddler . . . which a priest, a poet —

anonymously naked in the cyanide chambers ?

Who wept for them ?

Who shall remember them . . . where none was left

to weep or to remember ?

They died because.

Not even those who knew could understand.

Not as martyrs, exactly, or heroes . . . there was no virtue involved

or morals,

no guilt or innocence —

there were no public burnings at the stake, or crucifixions

for sculptors to memorialize,

for balladiers —

no tombs to enshrine,

no corpus delicti to exhibit,

no Thermopylae . . . or Gettysburg . . . or Stalingrad to dedicate —

their dying strengthened no earthly good, weakened no evil —

proved nothing, taught nothing . . . began or ended nothing.

3

On every wall of a room, in every room of a house,
in every house in Bavaria —
a humble, wounded, dying Jew-Christ on a cross.

Cast, carved, painted Jew-Christ on every wall
in Bavaria . . . in every corner,
Jew-angels,
wise bearded Jews partaking of the Last Supper,
the Jewess, Mary . . . with smiling little Jew-God.

I cannot understand this.

The gas chambers of Maidanek had walls, too.
And there were hooks for life-size images
on the bloodied walls of Belsen and of Dachau.

4

Spring in the Villa Sonnental.

The young plum tree between
the stripped chimney and a crumbled wall
blossoms warm white like a girl dressed for her wedding.

In the gardener-less garden
the ivy ventures slenderly like young green snakes
upon the tiled walk.

The variegated vines gather unto themselves
the bronze and stone Teutonic faces —
camouflage the irritating challenge of Bismarck . . . claim
the coy nudes by the swimming pool filled with brown rain water.

The thrush with his love and a brand new summer home
in the jasmine bush
sings an impromptu matinee to an empty house.

Festung Koenigstein squats ponderously atop like a marble
mountain, split and reassembled
the Teutonic way —
with slits for archers and deep dungeons for darkness and fear.

It has no beauty in itself . . . its only beauty is
what can be seen below,
what lies within the reach, the azimuth of the eye —
left there by humbler men . . . by older, unrecorded ages:

the wooded hills and the orange-shingled villages
cupped between —
the stream, silverly sinuous as the captured pattern
of a lighthearted shepherd's song.
Time-toned crags and moss-tamed fences and walls.

Its only virtue is
that it is ruined . . . and its architects are dead —
though it is through their Moloch breed I am here to view it.

6

NOW IN MAY —

having buried the invader and the liberator, alike,
France is beautiful again.
Only the charred twisted bodies of tanks and carriers,
immune to the sun and the bluebottle,
still line the roadsides and litter the green, mine-denied plains.

Only the caved bridges too ponderous for the small flood waters
of the Moselle to sweep away.
The tangled parallels of rails, the heaped cities too vast to bury.

The crossroads Christ, decapitated to clear the field of fire.
The tall precise poplars, cut to deny the sniper his hiding.

But the land no longer mourns . . . the land never mourns long —
the fields renew each spring, the grass mends quickly.
The assiduous weeds rebuild, close darkly over the graves
and the craters,
over the Tellers and the shoemines and the bouncing Betties.
Heal over the unrecovered dead as the sea heals over drowned sailors.

The creeper and the ubiquitous ivy have tamed the barbed entanglements
into trellises
with the insistent undeniable tenderness of woman making love.

The wild blue delphinium . . . and the cornflower,

the red clover and white, the green wheat jeweled with cinnabar poppies,

flood the eye and honey the warm air.

7

Germany, the land that is Germany, has beauty, too.
The dark, green, ancient plains . . . the hills,
high-castled Heidelberg, forests of beach and pine,
the terraced vineyards on the steep banks of the Rhine —

the Rhine of Lorelei . . . the Rhine of the Nibelungs,
swirling over scuttled barges and backbroken bridges.

But the cities, shoveled off the streets, shelter the dead
sponsored on the air by the warm spring rain.
I saw fresh flowers and a cross on one of the many buried homes
in Aachen —
on the great grave that was Cologne an old woman kneeled praying.

The towers designed never to fall . . . fell.
The granite walls,
intended to grow green with moss and great with conquest,
crumbled in the vacuum of burst blockbusters.

The dugouts — tremendous, concrete redoubts —
soured with the stench of blood and nitro, lie
turned inside-out and silhouetted on the scarred vantage hills.

Those returning converge futilely upon the ruins —
the old, passive and sullen . . . the children, waving or nazi-saluting.
The older boys, having put away their daggers for another day,

sidestep the onrushing trucks leisurely, contemptuously.
Only the women . . . the young blue-eyed women, smile —
their infinite weapon is the warm promise of love.

Our driver, a kid from Iowa, admits he would love being conquered
by one of these, pedaling their bicycles uninhibited,
generous with their full, white thighs.

Lt. Marcus says: Christ ! It makes me sick, these people,
lost, tired . . . pushing their carts nowhere —

S/Sgt. Davis says: Lieutenant, if you feel like that,
why do you inspect your piece . . . and put one into the chamber
every night before you hit the sack ?
Okay, you won't like me . . . but I, for one, am proud of all this.
Because it had to be either Hamburg or New York, Dusseldorf
or Detroit . . . Heilbronner or Blue Ridge.
That old guy there under the tree . . . or maybe my father.

Lt. King, his face patched up with the skin off his side, says:
Marcus, did you ever get to go through Buchenwald ?
Were you ever in Belsen or Dachau . . . have you ever heard
of Lidice or Warsaw, Stalingrad, Rotterdam, Coventry . . . or seen
starved women and men . . . and children
gassed, drowned, poisoned, clubbed — hanged on the hooks and sent
still kicking down the conveyor into white-hot ovens ?

What do you think when you look at the empty sleeves
all over the world . . . the pinned-up pantlegs, the stitched
Frankenstein faces . . . like this —
the awful haunted eyes that will never know peace, even in peace ?

You should have followed us with the corpsmen through the woods
of Huertgen.
You should have gone from tank to tank with them in the hedgerows of
    Normandy,
Kasserine or the Bulge —
probing for identifying dogtags in the dark American ashes.

You should have tried surviving a torpedoed boat at night,
strafed, rammed, machinegunned in the oily flaming sea.

Their carts bother you ? Their lost tired look ?
There never was a people since the beginning that deserved
what they got
more than these did — may the good Lord forever damn the bastards !

8

Night skulking in the ruins of the city and the mind
gathers oppressively . . . odorous as a gangrenous wound.

Night without music or lovers, without light or compensatory dreams,
without certain tomorrow —
disturbing night,
like a face in the window or a bomb ticking in the near unknown.

What am I doing here ?

To slay in anger is light, even joyous . . . to slay the slayer
when vengeance or fear blacks out the brain
and the uniform makes blessed and honored murderers of all.

But when the enemy is: the gaunt old
walking like weeping Jeremiahs among the heaped and blackened homes;
and when the enemy is: rickety children big-eyed with hunger;

and when the enemy is: young girls bartering love
for a bar of candy
or a cigarette . . . a cup of coffee or a cot in a heated room;

and when the enemy is: the lost, the vacant —
the aimless something belched out of a vast and blind explosion;

I have no heart for that.
Mine is not the skill for overseeing.
My hand is not the hand to wield God's flaming sword.

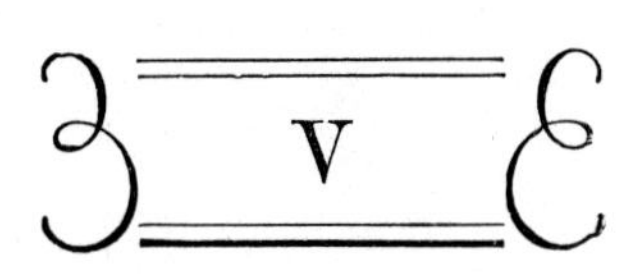
V

The Dead Are on the Air Tonight

Can you hear us ? Hello . . . can you hear us ?

It is one minute past time.
It is quiet here, facing the night . . . the dust is falling,
with no colors whatever and no sense to anything.

We arrived in heavy traffic
(converging from the earth's four corners) and entered
the infinite dimension as the blue enters the night.

Can anyone hear us ?

We found no Hallowe'en world with lean shapes and lantern
faces . . . no Tartarus nor Ultima Thule —
we found no evergreen land at the rainbow's end:

no mead and manna and broiled quail on wing to eat
and angel-girls to lay —
no wailing by the Stygian shore nor singing in the stars.

Nothing to compensate the meek or level the proud,
to reward the good or punish the evil —
to enrich the disinherited or impoverish the landlords of the earth

We found nothing, no one, nowhere, because
the way it happened was:
suddenly we reached an immense edge —

For Armistice

When about this time a commemorative group is unveiled,
a cenotaph opened for inspection —
observe the whippet bronze, the winged thew, the precise

rhythm . . . and think of the rehearsed dying it took
to model these splendid attitudes.
Only . . . some of us having seen men die, know they do not

die in adagio movement, poised thus . . . heroically,
to register the finest emotions,
the most typical national look . . . for the grand close-up.

Have you ever seen an original enshrined . . . unposed
and without make-up,
showing fear or resignation, bewilderment or shock —
with the carrion crow and the bluebottle for local color ?

The Unknown Soldier

After a round of madness and a vague
moment of pain . . . after forty winks of death, night came —

after a shuddering interval of dark, when a great hand
fell on the switch,
shorted the circuit, cut all the wires, blew out the main fuse.

And I was dredged out of the Rapido or the Rhine,
the Neckar, the Moselle,
recovered from the debris of Anzio or Aachen . . . Bastogne, St. Lo —
face leveled, dogtags blown off.

Charred past recognition in a gas-drenched tank.
Assembled in a shelter-half on the mined reef off Iwo Jima.
Went down. Failed to return.
Was reported lost.
Was entered missing in the morning report.

A body in the image of God was lying on the plain,
the maggot and the bluebottle cast dice for it
and black bald birds swung lower and lower for their cut.

Angels came out of their caves and lay on the ledges
sunning themselves . . . like old men or lepers —

And in the last world, quarrelsome old men
convened in domed halls and bannered parliaments to vote
for a vast, splendid, residential tomb.

Summary of the Distance between the Diving Bomber and the Objective

How slenderly space splits . . . the momentum doubles,
squares,
(precise, flawless as on paper)
the dynamite muscles flexed for sudden violence —
the electric key poised to unlock the plutonian vaults of fire!

Beautiful . . . beautiful to see against the sky
of flying birds —
against the soft, wide, lavender eyes of morning!

There, proud physicist, beauty enamoured poet,
miracle credulous priest . . . behold
the stark embodiment of the millennia of mind . . . mythic, mechanical —

Euclid's theorems, Phidias's chiseled curves,
The Flood, Redemption . . . and The Song of Songs,
Rembrandt, Beethoven, Steinmetz, Plato, Christ —

all the oldest principles . . . all the latest features
capsuled in a swift and shining shape
to blow man and his world out of context and material time.

The Preview

THE GHOUL-ANGELS WHO ANGELED THE LAST BIG SHOW ANNOUNCE

A NEW PRODUCTION —

A STIRRING SEQUEL TO THE RECENT MAKER OF STARS AND HEROES.

What say the impresarios . . . the commentators ?
Yes — what of the thinkers of our thoughts ?
The speakers of our lines ? The prompters ?
Who are the sponsors ? Who are the statesmen-to-be ?

The spotlight darts about like a lost pup
sniffing at every heel.
The spotlight wanders like a drunk amnesiac.

They are looking for a slogan, they are
looking for a title . . . they are looking for a cause.

They are casting now.
The props are ready. The boxoffice is manned.

Darkness whispers behind the curtain.
Fear watches from the wings with catching eyes.
Ominous music.
Someone smells smoke.

Somebody dies. Somebody dies. Somebody dies . . .

There Are No Good Giants

Once more the strong reach out. The weapons vary:
gold, gun . . . a missionary.
But the force is there, the force is always there,

the force of steel or an editorial . . . tribal, economic force,
topographical.
The persuasion of bread, as irresistible as knife held to the throat —
of dialectics, as convincing as God . . . or an atom bomb.

Once more the historic words, the slogans . . . the familiar
names that have bloodied man's record.
Oil. Dardanelles. Balance of power. Outlet to the sea.

The strong reach out in all directions, there are no good
giants . . . O believe this —
correct the fables, revise your children's nursery rhymes,
tell them it is wrong even for the good to be too strong.

Even a lover turns tyrant . . . with love's scepter for power.

Lines for Anyone

I can think of no moral . . . no prophecy to tell you.
I am a poet — not seer or evangelist.
I can neither see the shape of tomorrow in the lay of tea leaves
nor read prophetically between the lines of a dream.

Even as you. I am uncertain as you, thwarted, amazed,
evil or good as you . . . or neither good nor evil —

my fears are your fears, old fears . . . of want and loneliness,
of unknown tomorrow.
Of such death as war and lynchers bring,
of hate often taught and intolerance bequeathed and legislated —

my needs are your needs, old needs . . . of bread and love,
of work and peace,
of room to grow, and time to think, and long years to live —

I fail where you fail, seek what you would find . . . question
what you would have answered —
O will we ever know our rumored greatness

who kill as stonemen killed for one's tongue or color,
conscience or face of God,
with piety on our lips and science shining in our eyes —
embracing logic or the cross as an adulteress her husband.

Born in Austria of Russian parents, Walter Benton has lived most of his life in the United States. After working on a farm, in a steel mill, as a window washer, as a salesman, and at various other jobs, he entered Ohio University in 1931, and in due course was graduated. He then spent five years as a social investigator in New York. During the second World War he served in the United States Army, being commissioned a lieutenant of the Signal Corps in the autumn of 1942 and later being promoted to a captaincy. He has now returned to New York, where he is devoting his time to writing. Never a Greater Need, *a selection of the best poems he has written since the publication of* This is My Beloved *in 1943, was issued in 1948.*

This book was set on the Linotype in Bodoni Book, *a printing-type so called after Giambattista Bodoni, a celebrated printer and type designer of Rome and Parma* (1740–1813). Bodoni Book *as produced by the Linotype company is not a copy of any one of Bodoni's fonts, but is a composite, modern version of the Bodoni manner. Bodoni's innovations in printing-type style were a greater degree of contrast in the " thick and thin " elements of the letters, and a sharper and more angular finish of details.*

The book was composed by The Plimpton Press, Norwood, Massachusetts, and printed and bound by H. Wolff, New York. Typography and binding based on designs by W. A. Dwiggins.